BREAKING THE CHAINS OF BONDAGE

by

Billy Joe Daugherty

Breaking the Chains of Bondage
ISBN 1-56267-130-8
Copyright © 1999 by
Billy Joe Daugherty
Victory Christian Center
7700 South Lewis Avenue
Tulsa, OK 74136-7700

BREAKING THE CHAINS OF BONDAGE

CONTENTS

INTRODUCTION

Jesus Christ, the Anointed One **"...was manifested, that He might destroy the works of the devil"** (1 John 3:8). He came to undo what Satan has done. Jesus came to reverse the curse and to bring God's blessings of salvation; health and wholeness; soundness of mind; a happy marriage, home, and family; and financial and spiritual prosperity into your life.

You have a role to play to break the chains of bondage in your life and to maintain your freedom. In the teaching in this book, *Breaking the Chains of Bondage,* the areas of bondage and their root cause are identified, then you will learn "how to" break free and stay free of these demonic strongholds.

This is the hour when you must walk in total freedom in Christ so you can run with the vision God has given you and set other captives free.

In John 8:34-36, Jesus said:

> **"Most assuredly, I say to you, whoever commits sin is a slave of sin.**
>
> **"And a slave does not abide in the house forever, but a son abides forever.**
>
> **"Therefore if the Son makes you free, you shall be free indeed."**

Sin is the root cause of all bondage. Jesus Christ paid the cost in full with His shed blood to set you free from every chain of bondage and to keep you free.

My prayer for you is that you will receive the completed work of His death, burial, and resurrection and experience His liberation as you meditate upon and obey the biblical principles for absolute freedom found in these pages.

Billy Joe Daugherty

1

THE MINISTRY OF JESUS: DESTROYING THE WORKS OF THE DEVIL

After Jesus' baptism by John the Baptist in the Jordan and His forty days of fasting, followed by the temptations of the devil, He stood up in the synagogue of His home town of Nazareth and began His ministry by reading from the book of Isaiah:

> "The Spirit of the Lord is upon Me, because He has anointed Me to preach the gospel to the poor; He has sent Me to heal the brokenhearted, *to proclaim liberty to the captives* and recovery of sight to the blind, to set at liberty those who are oppressed;
>
> "To proclaim the acceptable year of the Lord."
>
> Then He closed the book, and gave it back to the attendant and sat down. And the eyes of all who were in the synagogue were fixed on Him.
>
> **Luke 4:18-20**

The Living Bible says Jesus was sent **"...to announce that captives shall be released...."** *The Amplified Bible* says Jesus was sent **"...to announce release to the captives...."**

"To proclaim the acceptable year of the Lord"

1

refers to the year of Jubilee – the fiftieth year after seven, seven-year periods. The year of Jubilee was a year of total freedom to all the inhabitants of Israel – debts were canceled; possessions were regained; food was plentiful; safety prevailed in their land; abundant provision was available to the poor; and hired servants were set free.

Jesus said, **"Today this Scripture is fulfilled in your hearing"** (Luke 4:21). He was saying, "I am the Jubilee." *Jubilee* is a picture of Christ Who sets the captives free, cancels the debt of sin, and brings God's abundance and blessings into our lives.

Jesus was proclaiming, "I am the Anointed One, the One God raised up to bring deliverance." Those in the synagogue were so angry with Jesus they rose up with the intent to throw Him off the cliff and run Him out of town. Verse 30 says, **"Then passing through the midst of them, He went His way."**

Jesus came **"...that He might destroy the works of the devil"** (1 John 3:8) and to set us free. In John 8:36 Jesus said, **"Therefore if the Son makes you free, you shall be free indeed."**

Jesus came to undo what Satan had done. He came to reverse the curse and bring God's blessings of salvation; health and wholeness; soundness of mind; a happy marriage, home, and family; and financial and spiritual prosperity into our lives.

2

Breaking the Chains of Bondage Confession

Speak this confession aloud, believe it in your heart, and begin to act as if it is already true in your life:

Since Jesus Christ of Nazareth is the Jubilee of my life, I experience the benefits of Jubilee every day. Through His completed work at Calvary, Jesus paid the price for my deliverance from sin and its bondage; He paid for the healing and wholeness of my body, mind, and spirit; He paid for my provision which includes His blessings without sorrow; and He paid for eternal life for me, as well as my spiritual well-being.

Because Jesus already destroyed the works of the devil, I can walk free of the chains of bondage by bringing my life in line with the standard of God's Word. Jesus provided freedom from all the works of the enemy, and whom He sets free is free indeed! In Jesus, I am free indeed!

(See Proverbs 10:22; Luke 4:18-20; 1 John 3:8; John 8:36.)

Chapter Review

As you review the teaching in this chapter, please fill in the blanks of the statements/questions below:

1. In Luke 4:18-20, Jesus' character, His call, and His purpose are summarized. As a born-again, Spirit-filled believer, your life is to be modeled after His character, call, and purpose:

    a. The _____ of the Lord is upon me.

    b. I am _____ to preach (to share) the gospel.

    c. I am sent to _____ the brokenhearted.

    d. I am anointed to proclaim _____ to the captives.

    e. I am anointed to bring _____ _____ _____ to the blind (this could include both natural and spiritual blindness).

    f. I am to set at _____ those who are oppressed.

    g. I am to proclaim the acceptable year of the Lord. In other words, I am to introduce others to the _____, the Lord Jesus Christ.

2. _____ is the Anointed One.

4

3. Jesus came to _____ the works of the devil (1 John 3:8).

4. To be set free by Jesus Christ the Son means to be made _____ indeed (John 8:36).

2

IDENTIFYING AREAS OF BONDAGE

Millions of people are enslaved by some type of bondage. To be in *bondage* means to be enslaved or subjected to some force, compulsion, or influence; to be under the control or manipulation of something evil and destructive; to be led away from God's best and the path He has ordained for you to walk, keeping you from fulfilling all that He has called you to do.

A person could be in bondage to wrong thoughts, a philosophy, an attitude, an emotion, feelings, or actions.

If you are led by your flesh rather than by the Holy Spirit, here are some of the works of the flesh which will bring you into bondage:

> **Now the works of the flesh are evident, which are: adultery, fornication, uncleanness, lewdness,**
>
> **Idolatry, sorcery, hatred, contentions, jealousies, outbursts of wrath, selfish ambitions, dissensions, heresies,**
>
> **Envy, murders, drunkenness, revelries, and the like; of which I tell you beforehand, just as I also told you in time past, that those who practice such things will not inherit the kingdom of God.**
>
> **Galatians 5:19-21**

The Living Bible describes the works of the flesh as:

...Impure thoughts, eagerness for lustful pleasure,

Idolatry, spiritism (that is, encouraging the activity of demons), hatred and fighting, jealousy and anger, constant effort to get the best for yourself, complaints and criticisms, the feeling that everyone else is wrong except those in your own little group – and there will be wrong doctrine,

Envy, murder, drunkenness, wild parties, and all that sort of thing. Let me tell you again as I have before, that anyone living that sort of life will not inherit the Kingdom of God.

Some people are bound by cigarettes, drugs, and alcohol, which systematically destroy the body. An elderly lady in our church had been smoking since she was a teenager. She was set free after more than fifty years of smoking. Over a period of years, she spent thousands of dollars blowing smoke!

Other areas of bondage include worry, anxiety, laziness, and gambling. Many people are hooked on the lottery, thinking one ticket will make them a millionaire. Many times money is spent for bingo or lottery tickets that should have been used for meeting the needs of the children in the family.

Some people are in bondage to money. They just can't get enough. Others are in bondage to shopping. As they drive by the mall, their car automatically turns in!

Another area of bondage often overlooked is the

workaholic. This person may be a Christian who loves God, but he or she is so committed to their work that they begin to neglect their spiritual life and family. An erosion takes place until the foundation of their spiritual life crumbles or their marriage falls apart, all because of an obsession with economic success.

I believe in being the best you can be, but not to the exclusion of God or your family. If you gain the whole world, but lose your own soul, what will it profit you? If you gain everything and yet lose your family, you won't have a lot of fun sitting alone with all your toys! Many people are in this situation today.

Proverbs 10:22 says, **"The blessing of the Lord makes one rich, and He adds no sorrow with it."** The true blessings of God will not cause you to sacrifice your relationship with Him. God's prosperity and success will not destroy, but they will enrich. They will give you joy instead of ulcers. They will give you victory instead of depression. Many people have climbed to the peak of success, as the world describes it, only to find a plateau of emptiness.

Keep Your Focus on Jesus

To break out of the chains of bondage of the flesh and to maintain your freedom, you must keep your focus on Jesus. Or, we could say it this way: Keep the main thing in your life — Jesus — the main thing!

In Colossians 3:1-10, Paul says it this way:

If then you were raised with Christ, seek those things

which are above, where Christ is, sitting at the right hand of God.

Set your mind on things above, not on things on the earth.

For you died, and your life is hidden with Christ in God.

When Christ who is our life appears, then you also will appear with Him in glory.

Therefore put to death your members which are on the earth: fornication, uncleanness, passion, evil desire, and covetousness, which is idolatry.

Because of these things the wrath of God is coming upon the sons of disobedience,

In which you yourselves once walked when you lived in them.

But now you yourselves are to put off all these: anger, wrath, malice, blasphemy, filthy language out of your mouth.

Do not lie to one another, since you have put off the old man with his deeds,

And have put on the new man who is renewed in knowledge according to the image of Him who created him.

There is no lasting fulfillment in life outside of a relationship with Jesus Christ.

Why Be Ruled by the Holy Spirit?

Bondages rob people of the goodness and blessings of God. They steal, kill, and destroy, which is the description

Jesus gave in John 10:10 of the devil's works. Bondages destroy health, mental sanity, marriages and families, careers, and the destiny God has ordained for you to fulfill.

God's will is that we allow the Holy Spirit to control every aspect of our lives. The work of the Holy Spirit in the human spirit will produce **"...love, joy, peace, long-suffering, kindness, goodness, faithfulness, gentleness, self-control..."** (Galatians 5:22,23).

Verse 24 says, **"And those who are Christ's have crucified the flesh with its passions and desires."** To *crucify* means to put to death or destroy. In other words, to *crucify* the flesh means to put to death the works of the flesh. Verse 25 says, **"If we live in the Spirit, let us also walk in the Spirit."**

In verse 21 Paul said that those who practice the works of the flesh **"...will not inherit the kingdom of God."** Some people say, "You can live any way you want and still inherit the Kingdom of God." That's like saying, "We are going to let murderers loose in City Hall!" No way! The person who is convicted of a crime is put away to protect the innocent.

In our city we have seen people with money, nice homes, big cars, and successful businesses and careers lose it all as they gunned down their spouse. How could this happen when everything in the natural looks so "right"? Did it just come on them in a moment? No, little bondages developed when they were children or teenagers that were never dealt with until the bondages became monsters. Then, in a moment of emotional rage, one of the monsters was unleashed and they did something they never dreamed they were capable of doing.

If you don't kill the monster, the monster will kill you. If you don't conquer the flesh, the flesh will conquer you.

In the natural realm, people who won't live by the law are put away. God follows this same principle. Some people say, "How could a loving God do that?" Because He loves the innocent, the righteous, and those who love Him. He isn't going to allow the works of the flesh and the devil to destroy His Kingdom.

Sharon and I have seen the devastating results of the works of the flesh in many lives, where the flesh was unrestrained until calamity, tragedy, or brokenness resulted. We have ministered in many places to those who are paying for the works of their unruly flesh.

We are in a serious hour. If there is a bondage in your life, no matter how insignificant it may seem to be, deal with it so Jesus can be Lord of every area of your life. The gospel has the power to set you free from every bondage.

Breaking the Chains of Bondage Confession

Speak this confession aloud, believe it in your heart, and begin to act as if it is already true in your life:

Through the power of the Holy Spirit within me, I

renounce every work of the flesh that has ensnared me so I can be free to run the race that Jesus has set before me. I will keep my focus on Jesus, the author and finisher of my faith, and I will run my race successfully and complete the destiny to which God has called me.

As I am daily washed with the water of God's Word, the works of my flesh are being replaced with the fruit of the Holy Spirit that are maturing in my spirit – love, joy, peace, longsuffering, kindness, goodness, faithfulness, gentleness, and self-control.

I'll be bound only to Christ as an obedient servant in God's Kingdom!

(See Hebrews 12:1,2; Ephesians 5:26; Galatians 5:22,23.)

Chapter Review

As you review the teaching in this chapter, please fill in the blanks of the statements/questions below:

1. List the works of the flesh that are a challenge to you right now that you are bringing into submission to the Holy Spirit. Beside each "work of the flesh" you list, give the Scripture reference(s) that you are believing and speaking to alleviate this work of the flesh:

   <u>Work of the Flesh</u>   <u>Scripture</u>

   _____   _____

   _____   _____

   _____   _____

   _____   _____

   _____   _____

   _____   _____

2. Previously, I have broken the chains of bondage in various areas of my life by _____

   _____

   _____

   _____

3. I am maintaining my freedom from the chains of bondage by_____

_____

_____

_____

_____

3

LIBERATION BEGINS WITH A CHOICE

You can be delivered from any type of bondage, but first you must make a choice that you want to be free.

Sharon prayed for a young lady in our church who was so entrenched in bondage that it seemed there was no way out – until she accepted the work of the true Liberator, Jesus Christ. Here is her letter to Sharon:

"God has performed so many miracles in my life this past year. I'm a 100 percent, totally new person. When Pastor Billy Joe was talking about joy recently, it was great knowing that I finally have it. I could relate very well to his happy hour story. I know what it's like to go into bars to drink with friends and get a few kicks, but you know, the kicks ended when I walked out the door and got in my car to go home alone.

"After you've been out drinking all night, you feel more alone when you get home than you did before you went. So what's the remedy? You drink when you get home, too, so you can go to sleep. Then you drink when you get up to forget last night, and then you drink again before you go out that night so you can have a good buzz going and already be happy when you see your friends.

"Before I knew it, I was a twenty-five-year-old alcoholic who smoked three packs of cigarettes a day. I was wined and dined in the best places money could buy. The only drawback was that I still went home alone every night to an empty apartment in which I spent many hours and many nights crying and throwing up. This is the wonderful single life that is portrayed in all the beer and cigarette commercials. Even flying to Europe five times a month with my job as an airline stewardess wasn't relieving any of the depression.

"Finally, last May I was put in the hospital for dehydration. I was supposed to be able to leave in two days, but when my blood work came back, they discovered my liver was failing. Two days stretched into two weeks. My doctor called all my family in to see me, because he didn't think I was going to make it through the night.

"Three weeks earlier, I was a twenty-five-year-old girl, supposedly having the time of my life. Now I'm a twenty-five-year-old girl who may not see tomorrow.

"After my family had gone home, my doctor's wife, who is a Spirit-filled Christian and a good friend of mine, came into my room to pray for me. I had never told her about my real lifestyle, but after she prayed, she told me that God had spoken to her, if I would get rid of the sin in my life, I would live. Of course, I said that I would, and by morning, my high enzyme count had dropped 50 percent and my temperature was gone. I left the hospital two days later.

"This was the middle of June, and I returned to work in mid August. Unfortunately, it took me a full year to get rid of all the sin in my life, but I did do it. It was ten times harder getting myself to where I should be, where I am now. Because I finally made up my mind and I was willing to work hard, I can now stand before you or anyone else and say, 'I am 100 percent free of witchcraft, alcohol, drugs, and cigarettes.' Not only can I say it to you, but I can look you in the eyes when I say it.

"Praise God, I'm finally free, free, free, free."

Sharon had prayed for this young lady a few years ago. She experienced a degree of freedom and confessed Christ, but bondages ensnared her after that. Believers can still have bondages clinging to their lives. Like this young lady, it is important to press on for *total freedom* in every area.

The first step to being liberated from bondage is, *you must desire to be free*. Freedom is available to those who want it. The two primary motivations behind the desire to be free, as well as behind most choices you will make, are:

- The benefits to be gained, and
- The losses to be avoided.

Imagine a twenty-five year old whose liver is failing. Alcohol was a bondage this young woman had become ensnared by because of a lifestyle on the fast track that was portrayed as exciting.

My son John, as a young boy, in our devotions compared it to a trap, baited to catch an animal. The trap has claws to catch its victim. Once it catches them, it holds them. So it is with the losses people experience after they have tasted the pleasure of sin for a season. The pleasure grabs them, and it turns into pain and heartache.

Sin always steals, kills, and destroys, whether it takes weeks, months, or years. No matter how beautiful it is packaged or how good it sounds, ultimately it will sting. It will rob you of life. *When you want to be free regardless of what it takes, you will be set free.*

There's a story of a young executive who went fishing with an older executive. The young man was admiring the success of the older gentleman. He asked, "How did you attain such great success? How did you build this great corporate empire?" The older man took hold of the young man, pulled him over the side of the boat, stuck his head under the water and held him there. When it appeared that the young man was about to drown, the older gentleman pulled him up and said, "When you want success like you wanted that breath of air, you will get it!"

When you want freedom from bondage more than anything else in life, you will get it!

Breaking the Chains of Bondage Confession

Speak this confession aloud, believe it in your heart, and begin to act as it is already true in your life:

Father, I choose to be totally delivered from every type

of bondage that has ensnared me so I am free to mount up with wings like an eagle; so I can run and not be weary; and so I can walk victoriously and not faint. I want to be free so I can be a champion in Your Kingdom.

(See Isaiah 40:28-31.)

Chapter Review

As you review the teaching in this chapter, please fill in the blanks of the statements/questions below:

1. The most important step that I must take to be free of bondage is _____

   _____

2. I choose to be totally free of _____

   _____

3. I believe Jesus wants me free because _____

   _____

   _____

   _____

4

IDENTIFYING THE ROOT CAUSE OF BONDAGES

Once the desire to be free of bondage exists, it's time to identify the *root cause* of those things that have held you in bondage.

The root cause of worry and anxiety often appears to be insecurity as a result of things that happened while a person was growing up.

The root cause behind the drive for materialism in many people appears to be the lack they experienced when they were growing up, the fear that if they don't stockpile and hoard, they won't have enough.

Many people are caught in the trap of immorality, uncleanness, and pornography because of emptiness in their life.

The root cause behind any kind of bondage could be emptiness, insecurity, a lack of acceptance, or something that happened in a person's childhood. However the real root cause for bondage of any type is *sin*.

When Adam and Eve partook of the forbidden fruit in the garden, Adam blamed Eve, Eve blamed the snake, and the snake had no one else to blame. Some people say,

"I came from a dysfunctional family. I had this problem, this lack, or this situation." The bottom line is, *God's law was broken in some way*. Until a person is brutally honest and willing to admit, "I have sinned," there will be no true liberation.

Many an alcoholic has been bound by his own thoughts and words: "I don't have a problem. I can quit any time I want to." It's the same way with the person who is a worrier who says, "I'm not fearful."

First John 1:9 says, **"If we confess our sins, He is faithful and just to forgive us our sins and to cleanse us from all unrighteousness."** You have to be brutally honest and admit, "I violated Your laws, Lord. I have done wrong."

It is one thing to be forgiven of an act, but it is another thing to be cleansed of the unrighteousness that caused the act. That's why First John 1:9 covers both areas:

- Forgiveness of the sin, and
- Cleansing from all unrighteousness.

Some people are looking only for temporary relief from guilt, but they don't want to deal with the root problem. The axe must be laid to the root to be free as God intends you to be.

In working with a young man who was an abuser, he admitted that he had never dealt with anger. His anger was caused by pride and arrogance. As a result of this "little bondage" – just a temper tantrum which probably started when he was a little boy and no one ever dealt with it – the day came when his wife, with four children all under ten years of age, said, "I've had it. Here are the divorce papers. It's over."

In a Wednesday evening church service, I had a word of knowledge for another man who was about to lose his marriage over anger that had never been dealt with. The word of the Lord was, "You have been blaming your wife for things, finding all of her faults, and you are about to leave her, but the real problem is in you. You have never dealt with the anger that is in your life. If you are repentant, God will cleanse you of that unrighteousness and remove it from your life. Then He will restore the marriage relationship and the love in your home."

First John 3:8 says, **"For this purpose the Son of God was manifested, that He might destroy the works of the devil."** There are works that are trying to destroy you. You will either conquer them or they will conquer you.

Colossians 1:13,14 says:

> **He [Jesus] has delivered us from the power of darkness and conveyed us into the kingdom of the Son of His love,**
>
> **In whom we have redemption through His blood, the forgiveness of sins.**

Jesus paid for your sin with His blood in His death, burial, and resurrection. He freed you from every bondage of Satan that would ever try to attach itself to you. Why does a person continue to remain bound once he or she accepts Christ and knows deliverance from every bondage has been paid in full? Either they don't know the truth, they refuse to believe it, or they don't stay with the process of renewing their mind with the Word and submitting their body to Jesus Christ.

You have to know that Jesus Christ has set you free to live free and then to set others free. The entire purpose of my life is *to live for God's glory, to be conformed to the image of Jesus Christ, and to give His life to other people.* This should be the purpose of every believer, though your witness may take place in a car dealership, an insurance office, at the mall, in your neighborhood, or while working at home.

It's time to address the chains, cords, and bondages that are holding your life, because it's difficult to set someone else free if you aren't free.

The writer of Hebrews says:

> **Let us strip off anything that slows us down or holds us back, and especially those sins that wrap themselves so tightly around our feet and trip us up; and let us run with patience the particular race that God has set before us.**
>
> **Hebrews 12:1 TLB**

Breaking the Chains of Bondage Confession

Speak this confession aloud, believe it in your heart, and begin to act as if it is already true in your life:

Father, in Jesus' name, I let go of all the former things that have happened in my life – both the good and the bad – that would limit what You desire to do in my life right now. I forgive and release everyone who has hurt me or hindered my walk with You. I release Your grace and mercy upon them, and I ask You to bless them, Lord.

I accept Your new plans for my life, Lord, which will spring forth quickly. Thank You for making roads in my wilderness and rivers in the desert of my life. Nothing is impossible with You, Lord.

Repentance on my part releases a cleansing by Your shed blood and a continual input of Your Word washes me and transforms me into Your image and likeness, Father. Thank You for freeing me from sin – the root cause of all bondage.

(See Isaiah 43:18,19; Luke 1:37; Ephesians 5:26).

Chapter Review

As you review the teaching in this chapter, please fill in the blanks of the statements/questions below:

1. The root cause of all bondage is _____.

2. If I confess my sins, God is faithful and just to _____ me of my sins and to _____ me from all unrighteousness (see 1 John 1:9).

3. Some of the enemy's works that have tried to destroy me are _____

   _____

   _____

   _____

   I am being totally liberated from these works by ____

   _____

   _____

   _____

   _____

4. To me, Jesus' death, burial, and resurrection mean

   _____

   _____

5

THE DESTRUCTIVENESS OF BONDAGES

Here are five of Satan's destructive goals for encouraging the development of bondages in your life:

First, God has a plan for your life, and bondages often come to keep you from fulfilling His plan.

I heard about a man who became bitter at a minister. Since his wife wanted to go to church, he would go with her, but he took books to read while the minister was preaching. Something had happened in the ministry and this man took it out on the minister. Although he didn't realize it at the time, he really was taking it out on the Head of that ministry, Jesus Christ. In the process he alienated himself from God.

Though he had a vision and a dream for his life and he was attempting to pursue it, he was held up by a little bondage called a grudge or resentment. Some people would call it unforgiveness, bitterness, wrath, or strife.

He said, "I watched my dream and vision completely disintegrate. It came to the point where our family didn't even have food to eat. That's when I began to pray and ask God what was wrong. The Lord showed me that I had held on to bitterness and resentment."

This man repented and today he is fulfilling God's plan for his life. Had he not changed the course of his life through repentance, God's plan would have remained on hold.

Romans 11:29 says, **"For the gifts and the calling of God are irrevocable."** *The King James Version* says, **"For the gifts and calling of God are without repentance."** If you break out of the bondages that are holding your life, you can fulfill God's call on your life.

Second, as a born-again believer, you are a reflection of the very life and glory of God. The only way Satan can strike back at God is to strike at you, God's creation.

Bondages often affect people's lives in such a way that instead of reflecting God's glory, they reflect a warped picture of God. You can't reflect the beauty, joy, love, and glory of Jesus if some bondage has bound your mind or body.

Third, another reason bondages develop is to stop you from setting other people free. We have been called to be co-laborers with God. When your chains are broken, then you can help set others free.

God has a bigger plan for you than just having you warm a church pew on Sunday morning! It's great if you are attending church regularly, but His plan goes far beyond once a week attendance. His plan is for you to release captives and touch them with His love everywhere you go. God wants *you* to be a liberator for Him.

If you have come out of a bondage, it is important that

you get a continual concentration of the Word of God. A little dab won't do you! You need the whole of God's glory, anointing, and presence to pour over you. This is one of the reasons we have Victory Bible Institute where people can overdose on God's Word.

Fourth, bondages often develop when people indiscriminately seek to fill the emptiness in their lives. The only way to fill the void of emptiness is with the presence of the Holy Spirit.

One of the bondages people use to fill the emptiness in their lives is soap operas. Another area is depressing music: "My baby left me.... My pickup died.... Dead skunk in the middle of the road!" Then some people become couch potatoes, and they just can't get away from the TV.

Some of the good habits that will strengthen your life are Christian music, God's Word, worship, prayer, and witnessing.

Fifth, other bondages develop when people succumb to temptation. Years ago I went into a nursing home to pray for the people. One lady asked me to get her snuff for her. I asked her, "Would you like me to pray for you to be free from it?" She got angry and didn't want me messing with her snuff! Sometimes people would rather have their bondages than Jesus.

First John 2:15-17 says:

> **Do not love the world or the things in the world. If anyone loves the world, the love of the Father is not in him.**

> For all that is in the world – the lust of the flesh, the lust of the eyes, and the pride of life – is not of the Father but is of the world.
>
> And the world is passing away, and the lust of it; but he who does the will of God abides forever.

James 1:13,14 reveals the origination of temptation:

> Let no one say when he is tempted, "I am tempted by God"; for God cannot be tempted by evil, nor does He Himself tempt anyone.
>
> But each one is tempted when he is drawn away by his own desires and enticed.

Temptation doesn't come from God. It comes from evil desire. When a person's wrong desires are stirred, he or she is drawn away and enticed. *Enticed* means to tempt, attract, allure, or draw into. *Conceived* means to give birth to. When lust has conceived and run its full course, it brings forth sin. Sin is the breaking of God's law, missing the mark, or failing to do what God has said. When sin is finished, it brings forth death.

This is what happened to Adam and Eve in the garden. Eve saw that the fruit was good to eat. She heard the devil lie and say she wouldn't die. The fruit was tantalizing to the eyes and then the devil said, "It will make you wise." Lust conceived. She listened to his lies and didn't respond to them with the truth. She started with the truth, but she didn't hold on to it.

It is possible to have the truth of God's Word in an area and yet not hold it to fight against wrong thoughts. When the evil desire conceives, sin is the result, and sin then brings forth death. Death is the absence of the life of God, separation from God, the loss of righteousness, the loss of authority and the blessings of God.

Christian leaders and lay people alike are going through the same temptations. No one is above temptation.

When a person repeats an action that is against God, it becomes a habit or a bondage. Then the devil lies to them and says, "This is the way life is. You must be content with your chains and bondages." Then comes guilt and condemnation. When you continue to break God's laws, the bondage becomes stronger.

The good news is, God will make a way to escape from the bondage of temptation if you are willing to receive the truth. If you keep messing with sin, however, guilt and condemnation will bring oppression. This is the very reason many people are on uppers and downers. They can't sleep and they don't have peace because of guilt. They've got to have something that will knock them out to sleep and then something to energize them during the day.

Guilt and condemnation rob people of motivation, energy, and drive. A cycle exists in which people fall deeper and deeper into the darkness of oppression.

First Corinthians 10:13 says:

> **No temptation has overtaken you except such as is common to man; but God is faithful, who will not allow you to be tempted beyond what you are able, but with**

the temptation *will also make the way of escape,* **that you may be able to bear it.**

Satan will tempt you in the same areas he tempted Adam and Eve and Jesus: the lust of the flesh, the lust of the eyes, and the pride of life. He may use new packaging, but his deals and the consequences of them have never changed! Look for the way of escape God has provided for you. You can overcome!

Breaking the Chains of Bondage Confession

Speak this confession aloud, believe it in your heart, and begin to act as if it is already true in your life:

Father, in Jesus' name I bind and put away all bitterness, wrath, anger, clamor, evil speaking, and malice from my life and I loose and receive Your kindness, tenderness, forgiveness, mercy, and grace into my life.

I am free from the bondages of Satan so I can set others free and so my life can be a reflection of your life, light, and love, Lord Jesus.

I resist temptation and I endure hardship as a good soldier of Jesus Christ. I will no longer be entangled by the affairs of this life, because I want to be totally free so I can please Him Who enlisted me as a soldier in His army!

(See Ephesians 4:31,32; James 4:7; 2 Timothy 2:3,4.)

Chapter Review

As you review the teaching in this chapter, please fill in the blanks of the statements/questions below:

1. I will no longer be entangled in bondage because God's plan for my life must be fulfilled. That plan is _____

    _____

    _____

    _____

    _____

2. The only way Satan can strike at God is to strike at God's _____.

3. I desire to set other people free from Satan's bondages because _____

    _____

    _____

    _____

    _____

4. To avoid a sense of "emptiness" in my life, I _____

    _____

    _____

_____

_____

5. The three descriptions of the spirit of the world found in First John 2:16 are

a. _____

b. _____

c. _____

6. No one is free of temptation, but I can escape it by ___

_____

_____

_____

_____

6

How To Break Free of the Chains of Bondage

Through the power of the Holy Spirit, you can be set free from any kind of bondage. In this chapter, I want to share with you some of the primary principles for breaking free of the bondages that have held you captive.

First, believe the Word of God that says you can be free. If your parents and grandparents have been in bondage, maybe you have begun to believe, "That's just the way it is. It's their personality traits. Because they are that way, I'll probably always be that way, too."

When you are born again, you become a new creation in Christ Jesus (2 Corinthians 5:17). The old traits and habits which were a reflection of Satan's nature have to go. You can come out of the muck and mire you have been in. You can live above the yoke of the devil's bondage. There is hope in Jesus.

> **And you shall know the truth, and the truth shall make you free...**
>
> **Therefore if the Son makes you free, you shall be free indeed.**
>
> **John 8:32,36**

Jesus will make you completely free in your spirit, soul, and body.

Second, make a decision that you will be free. Freedom is a choice. Choose to believe God's Word.

Joshua said, **"Choose for yourselves this day whom you will serve...But as for me and my house, we will serve the Lord"** (Joshua 24:15). Isaiah 1:19 says, **"If you are willing and obedient, you shall eat the good of the land."**

Third, humble yourself before the Lord and ask for His help. James 4:6 says, **"God resists the proud, but gives grace to the humble."** *Grace* is God's help. You will never be free from bondage without God's help. Your deliverance won't come by pulling your own boot straps up or by all the self-help things you can do. Jesus Christ, the author and finisher of your faith, is the only One Who can break the chains of bondage that have held you captive.

When I was growing up, we used to sing the song, "I Need Thee Every Hour." Every moment we need Jesus and His help, and through communion with the Holy Spirit, we can have His help! You can depend upon Jesus and rest upon all of the promises of God's Word.

The anointing of God, which is the release of God's power and presence, breaks the yoke of bondage (see Isaiah 10:27). Another way of saying it is, light drives out darkness, or the greatness of God will destroy the badness of the devil.

Fourth, get the anointed prayer and ministry of other believers who are full of the power of God. Have enough sense to know that if you are drowning, you need to call for help.

James said the sick should call for the elders of the church to pray over them and anoint them with oil in the name of the Lord (James 5:14). If you want to be set free from bondages, this same principle will work for you.

Fifth, fill yourself with the light of God's Word.

Jesus said:

When an unclean spirit goes out of a man, he goes through dry places, seeking rest, and finds none.

Then he says, "I will return to my house from which I came." And when he comes, he finds it empty, swept, and put in order.

Then he goes and takes with him seven other spirits more wicked than himself, and they enter and dwell there; and the last state of that man is worse than the first....

Matthew 12:43-45

Once you are set free, fill yourself up with God's Word on a daily basis so there is "no vacancy" for any work of the devil to enter you again. You can't just park and get a little bit on Sunday. If you are not putting forth energy against the powers of darkness, you will go backwards. That's why God gave us the picture of the children of Israel who had to get fresh manna *every morning.* We need fresh manna from heaven each morning, too. **"The entrance of Your words gives light..."** (Psalm 119:130).

People often do wrong things because of wrong thinking. Stinking actions come from stinking thoughts! To correct wrong thinking, you must saturate your mind with God's Word, which will renew your mind:

> **And do not be conformed to this world, but be transformed by the renewing of your mind, that you may prove what is that good and acceptable and perfect will of God.**
>
> **Romans 12:2**

The Lord said to Joshua:

> **This Book of the Law shall not depart from your mouth, but you shall meditate in it day and night, that you may observe to do according to all that is written in it. For then you will make your way prosperous, and then you will have good success.**
>
> **Joshua 1:8**

Daily meditation of the Word of God will keep it in your heart. With the Word spoken from your lips and the blood of the Lamb, Jesus Christ, that cleanses and keeps you, you will overcome the devil (Revelation 12:11).

Sixth, break off every wrong relationship that is feeding the bondage that has held you captive.

If you have had trouble with drinking, don't go to the bar to visit your buddies. First Thessalonians 5:22 says, **"Abstain from every form of evil."** If someone causes you to go into sin, don't call them up and say, "How are you doing?" Cut it off. If you've got a problem with anger, don't hang around angry people. Some people hang around circumstances that encourage their habits, not realizing it will cause the bondage to become even stronger.

If you are in an immoral relationship, break it off. The best way to break that type of relationship is don't say a word. Give no response – no letter, no call, no contact, no visit, and no explanation. Repent and let go of it, except if God leads you to say, "Forgive me. I repent of it and I forgive and release you."

If you don't take an immovable stand to break the relationship, it's easy to fall right back into it. Don't make plans to get together to talk it over again. Just break it off.

Seventh, become accountable to someone. Many a holy roamer in the church would have trouble being in a small group relationship where someone knows their name and looks them in the eye at least once a week and asks, "How are you doing?" They might find it challenging to have to be accountable to someone, but that's exactly what they need. Without this type of relationship, there is no accountability. In a small group where you are accountable, you can say, "I'm struggling in an area." Those around you can pray for you, believe God with you, and you can be free.

Many people try to be a lone ranger in their Christian walk. When you were born again, you were placed in the Body of Christ. Many people have been set free because believers gathered around them and continued to pray for them until the junk of their old life was off of them and out of them.

In Alcoholics Anonymous, a buddy system is in place that is highly effective. If you need help at any time, there is someone you can call who has been set free. Since this principle works in A.A., we ought to have enough sense to work the same principle in the Body of Christ.

Eighth, acknowledge that Jesus Christ already paid for your freedom with His blood.

When Jesus died on the cross and shed His blood, He paid in full for your release from Satan's bondages. Your chains were broken some 2,000 years ago. But until you get a vision of the victory of Calvary and the resurrection of Christ, you will never be totally free.

One of the greatest motivators to be free of bondage is to honor the blood that Jesus paid for your freedom. Jesus gave His blood for you to be free. To mock it by letting that bondage continue in your life without any resistance against it, is to disregard the blood of Jesus. It is to disregard the ministry of the Holy Spirit, Who will point you to the victory that Christ won and the righteousness that is available in Him.

Galatians 3:13,14 says Christ has already redeemed you from the curse of the law. Past tense! That means it's a "done deal"!

Christ has redeemed us from the curse of the law, having become a curse for us...

That the blessing of Abraham might come upon the Gentiles in Christ Jesus, that we might receive the promise of the Spirit through faith.

It is time to make a dedication of your life to live for God and to break every bondage off of your life so you can walk in continual freedom and victory. Make every effort to be free. If you stumble, get back up, repent, and go forward. Don't stay down and don't give up, for there is overcoming power in Jesus Christ. He believes in you and wants you loosed from the graveclothes of every type of bondage.

Breaking the Chains of Bondage Confession

Speak this confession aloud, believe it in your heart, and begin to act as if it is already true in your life:

I am a new creation in Christ Jesus. My old traits and habits have been replaced with the nature and attributes of Jesus Christ.

His nature is maturing in me as I spend time in study and meditation of God's Word, in prayer, in praise and worship of the Lord, and in fellowship with other believers of like spirit.

The truth of God's Word not only sets me free, but it keeps me free!

(See 2 Corinthians 5:17; Romans 12:1,2; John 8:32,36.)

Chapter Review

As you review the teaching in this chapter, please fill in the blanks of the statements/questions below:

1. I became a new creation in Christ Jesus when _____

   _____

   _____

   _____

2. The Anointed One and His _____ – Jesus Christ – break the chains of bondage that have held me captive (see Isaiah 10:27).

3. I am giving the devil and his works "no vacancy" in me so I can be free of all bondage and remain free of them by_____

   _____

   _____

   _____

   _____

4. According to Joshua 1:8, I am to meditate in God's Word day and night and then observe to obey all of it. The result will be that _____ and _____ come to me.

5. The purpose of accountability in the Body of Christ is

_____

_____

_____

_____

7

CONTINUAL WASHING WITH THE WATER OF THE WORD

If you abide in My word, you are My disciples indeed.

And you shall know the truth, and the truth shall make you free.

John 8:31,32

Verse 31 in the *King James Version* says, **"If ye** *continue* **in my word, then are ye my disciples indeed."** To *continue* means that you hear, believe, declare, obey, and abide in the Word. This is the same thought Jesus expressed in John 15:7: **"If you abide in Me, and My words abide in you, you will ask what you desire, and it shall be done for you."**

A *disciple* is one who continues in study and meditation of the Word of God. When we are "doing" God's Word, we are reproducing it in the lives of others. A disciple learns for the purpose of imparting what they have learned into someone else. Jesus had a very specific purpose in mind for His disciples and that was that they would reproduce themselves in others.

God's plan from the very beginning was that once He

saved us, He would use us to extend His Kingdom throughout the earth – preaching, teaching, healing, and ministering – from whatever platform He gives us – as an electrician, an accountant, a secretary, a teacher, a business person, in the neighborhood, the school, or wherever we are.

As you *continue* in God's Word and let the Word abide in you, it will fill you with the knowledge of God's will and liberate you from every bondage.

Sharon and I have seen people who were involved in drinking, drugs, cigarettes, compulsive gambling, immorality, and other bondages when they were born again, but as the Word got inside of them, their bondages fell off. If you will continue in God's Word, *the bondages will quit you,* because they don't want to hang around all that light, glory, and freedom!

John 17:3 describes eternal life as *knowing* God and His Son Jesus Christ – not just knowing about them, but knowing them intimately in a relationship where you are God's son or daughter and Jesus Christ is your Lord and Savior. Eternal life begins, not when you die physically, but the moment you accept Jesus Christ.

Second Peter 1:2 says, **"Grace and peace be multiplied to you in the knowledge of God and of Jesus our Lord."** *The more you know God the Father and Jesus Christ the Son, the more grace and peace will be multiplied in your life.*

As His divine power has given to us all things that pertain to life and godliness, through the knowledge of Him who called us by glory and virtue.

2 Peter 1:3

God's divine power, which is loosed in conjunction with our knowledge of Him, provides everything we need to live – mentally, emotionally, physically, financially, socially, and spiritually. Whether you need strength, nutrition, or spiritual weapons, God has already provided them for you. Whatever is lacking in your life, God has already provided it in Jesus Christ. That's why Paul wrote, **"And my God shall supply all your need according to His riches in glory by Christ Jesus"** (Philippians 4:19).

How then do we tap into the actual provision of all the things God has provided for us naturally and spiritually? Second Peter 1:4 contains the answer:

By which have been given to us exceedingly great and precious promises, that through these you may be partakers of the divine nature, *having escaped the corruption that is in the world through lust.*

As a result of God's great and precious promises, we become partakers of His divine nature – His joy, peace, victory, glory, and presence; and we escape all the corruption that is in this world. In other words, through God's Word we will escape the consequences of the corruption that works in the hearts and lives of people who are without God.

It's time to make God's promises the foundation of

your life. With at least 7,000 promises in the Word of God that are yours personally, there are enough to keep you busy for eternity and to provide for you in every situation you are facing.

Second Corinthians 1:20 says, **"For all the promises of God in Him are Yes, and in Him Amen, to the glory of God through us."**

One famous evangelist, E. Stanley Jones, said that all of God's promises find their "divine yes" in Jesus! In other words, Jesus came to say "yes" to life, wholeness, health, victory, and triumph. He didn't come to bring humanity a big "no." He came to bring us a great big "yes" from God!

One of God's promises, or benefits, is that He delivers us from destruction (Psalm 103:4). Not only does this include natural destruction such as earthquakes, hurricanes, tornadoes, and accidents, but it also includes the destruction that comes from sin, rebellion, and disobedience.

Through God's promises, we can be cleansed and perfected in holiness.

> **Therefore, having these promises, beloved, let us cleanse ourselves from all filthiness of the flesh and spirit, perfecting holiness in the fear of God.**
>
> **2 Corinthians 7:1**

Breaking the Chains of Bondage Confession

Speak this confession aloud, believe it in your heart, and begin to act as if it is already true in your life:

I abide in the Lord and His Word abides in me. As I continue to study and meditate upon God's Word daily, I am being cleansed by it and I am being prepared to become a reproducer of His life in others. As I continue in God's Word, Satan's bondages have no choice but to leave me.

It is through my relationship with the Father, Son, and Holy Spirit – and my knowledge of the Trinity through God's Word – that His divine power gives me all things that pertain to life and godliness.

I partake of God's divine nature by believing, speaking, and acting upon the promises of His Word.

(See John 8:31,32, 15:7; 2 Peter 1:2-4.)

Chapter Review

As you review the teaching in this chapter, please fill in the blanks of the statements/questions below:

1. I "continue" in God's Word by _____

   _____

   _____

   _____

2. I am making the promises of God's Word the foundation of my life by _____

   _____

   _____

   _____

3. I am being perfected in holiness by _____

   _____

   _____

   _____

8

INHERITING GOD'S PROMISES

How do we receive a manifestation of God's promises in the natural realm for both material and spiritual needs? Hebrews 6:12 contains the answer: **"Do not become sluggish, but imitate those who through *faith* and *patience* inherit the promises."**

Faith and *patience* are like wings on an airplane. You need both wings to fly. *Patience* is perseverance, endurance, steadfastness, staying with it, unchangeableness, and continuance.

Hebrews 11:1,2 describes *faith:*

> **Now faith is the substance of things hoped for, the evidence of things not seen.**

> **For by it the elders obtained a good testimony.**

God judges people by their faith in Him. Throughout the Bible, people were just as human as we are. They experienced great difficulties and did some horrible things, yet God called Abraham the father of our faith and He called David a man after His own heart.

God judged their hearts, and they had faith toward Him. When they made mistakes, they fell *forward*, trusting in God's grace. They didn't draw back from God, but kept believing. The goodness of God removes all of a person's sins of the past. Thank God for His mercy!

Joshua obtained a promise from God through faith and patience. One trip around the walls of Jericho for six consecutive days, seven trips around the wall on the seventh day, shout and blow the trumpets, and the walls fell. It took faith to tell his soldiers what they were to do, but it also took patience to stay with it for seven days when nothing changed outwardly.

Abraham had faith to leave his homeland, because God promised him a land and that He would make of him a great nation. God also told him He was going to give him a son, and through his son, all of the families of the earth would be blessed. But it was some twenty-five years before Isaac was born.

It took *faith* for Abraham to obey God and *patience* to stay with it. Romans 4:17-22 says of Abraham:

> (As it is written, "I have made you a father of many nations") in the presence of Him whom he believed – God, who gives life to the dead and calls those things which do not exist as though they did;

> Who, contrary to hope, in hope believed, so that he became the father of many nations, according to what was spoken, "So shall your descendants be."

> And not being weak in faith, he did not consider his own body, already dead (since he was about a hundred years old), and the deadness of Sarah's womb.

> He did not waver at the promise of God through

unbelief, but was strengthened in faith, giving glory to God,

And being fully convinced that what He had promised He was also able to perform.

And therefore "it was accounted to him for righteousness."

Abraham was fully persuaded that what God promised, He was able to perform. The promises of God will mean nothing to you unless you are fully persuaded that He is capable of performing them. This is why two people can sit side by side and one receives the manifestation of God's promises while the other receives nothing. The persuasion of the heart is a vital part of receiving. *When doubts and suspicions exist about the integrity of God's Word, faith is nullified.*

The traditions of men have made the Word of no effect in the lives of many people. When you remove the doubts and suspicions and settle it in your heart, like Abraham, giving glory to God, His promises will manifest. You can be fully persuaded that what God has promised, He will perform.

Psalm 37:4 says, **"Delight yourself also in the Lord, and He shall give you the desires of your heart."**

First John 5:14,15 says:

Now this is the confidence that we have in Him, that if we ask anything according to His will, He hears us.

And if we know that He hears us, whatever we ask,

we know that we have the petitions that we have asked of Him.

If God has already given a promise in His Word, then you can be assured it is His will. If it's in the Word, then it's a "yes" from God.

God is committed to His Word. He has exalted His Word above His name (Psalm 138:2). Why? Your name is only as good as your word. God is committed to His Word because He is a God of truth. He cannot lie. If He has spoken something, He will do it. Jesus said, **"Heaven and earth will pass away, but My words will by no means pass away"** (Matthew 24:35).

The Word was written by men who were inspired by the Holy Spirit. Second Timothy 3:16 says, **"All Scripture is given by inspiration of God, and is profitable for doctrine, for reproof, for correction, for instruction in righteousness."**

Faith

What is faith and how does it operate? Paul describes the spirit of faith in Second Corinthians 4:13, which is a repeat of Psalm 116:10: **"And since we have the same spirit of faith, according to what is written, *'I believed and therefore I spoke,'* we also believe and therefore speak."**

Paul repeated an Old Testament passage, because from one generation to another, the spirit of faith does not change. The faith that Noah exercised to build the ark, or Joshua to take the land of Canaan, or David to kill the giant, or Peter to be delivered from prison, right on down through history, is built on the same premise: *We believe and therefore we speak.*

Jesus revealed this same principle when He said, **"Out of the abundance of the heart the mouth speaks"** (Matthew 12:34). Proverbs 18:21 says, **"Death and life are in the power of the tongue, and those who love it will eat its fruit."** What the mouth speaks is an expression of the heart. It's time to *believe* and *speak* the promises of God.

Someone may ask you, "What are you going to do?" in a particular situation. You can respond, "I am going to *believe* and *speak* the promises of God."

God has a promise to cover every area of your life. Instead of using a negative report to express your feelings, hold fast to believing and speaking what God says in His Word. Only then will you inherit His promises.

Agree with God rather than with the devil. To "stand" on the promises means to agree with what God has already spoken. His Word is eternal. It will never change. Temporal things change from day to day, but God's Word is forever settled in heaven (Psalm 119:89). Jesus is the High Priest over these promises. He sees that they are carried out and fulfilled.

In Hebrews 4:1,2 God is speaking of the children of Israel who were slaves to the Egyptians, but God delivered them through ten miraculous signs. He parted the Red Sea for them, provided quail, manna, and water in the desert. Their shoes didn't wear out and their clothes didn't get old. Supernaturally, everything they needed was provided for them. God is still providing for His children today.

The Israelites were delivered when the death angel was loosed to destroy the oldest male child of every household because, in obedience to God, they sprinkled the blood of a lamb over their doorposts. The death angel couldn't touch a child in homes that were anointed with the blood of a lamb. This is symbolic of the effect of the blood of the Lamb, Jesus Christ.

Egypt was a type and shadow of the demonic bondages people are in today. Pharaoh represented the devil, and the Israelites were under his authority in a land of darkness, yet God delivered them. Their deliverance through the Red Sea is a type of water baptism. Their miraculous provision is a type of abundant life provided for us through Jesus Christ (John 10:10). The Israelites were covered with a cloud by day, that was a covering to guard against the intense heat, and a fire by night that protected them from the intense cold. Both the cloud and the fire represented the presence of the Holy Spirit.

Entering God's rest refers to entering the land of promise or the land of God's blessing.

Therefore, since a promise remains of entering His rest, let us fear lest any of you seem to have come short of it.

> **For indeed the gospel was preached to us as well as to them;** *but the word which they heard did not profit them, not being mixed with faith in those who heard it.*
>
> **Hebrews 4:1,2**

You must mix faith with the Word of God to inherit His promises. Your mixer is your heart and mouth. How do you mix faith with believing in your heart? Romans 10:17 says, **"So then faith comes by hearing, and hearing by the word of God."**

Since you are with you more than anyone else is with you, you are the best one to speak the promises to yourself each day. This is how you feed faith to your spirit. Believing and speaking God's promises is a continuous cycle. The more you believe the Word, the more you will speak it. The more you speak, the more you will believe.

We need to be so committed and locked into the Word of God that we won't be moved regardless of circumstances. In the fullness of time, the circumstances will change, *but the promises of God's Word will never change.*

Numbers 23:19 says:

> **God is not a man, that He should lie, nor a son of man, that He should repent. Has He said, and will He not do? Or has He spoken, and will He not make it good?**

It's time to stand on the promises for the salvation of your family members, for the health of your body, the sanity of your mind, the provision of finances, the anointing for boldness to witness, the authority over your emotions to control anger, fear, worry, and anxiety.

Mark 11:23 says:

For assuredly, I say to you, whoever says to this mountain, "Be removed and be cast into the sea," and does not doubt in his heart, but believes that those things he says will be done, he will have whatever he says.

The spirit of faith is expressed by speaking the Word to the mountains you are facing. If you are bound in an area, you can cut the cords of it through speaking the Word over that area. Turn on the light of the Word and watch the darkness flee!

Patience

Hebrews 10:23 KJV says, **"Let us hold fast the profession of our faith *without wavering*; (for he is faithful that promised)."**

Don't change your confession just because circumstances change. Don't change your stand just because your feelings sag or because of the opinions of others. Instead, set your face like a flint. Don't be moved to the right or to the left. Hold fast to the promises of God's Word.

There is a balance that needs to be achieved in taking your stand on God's Word and that is, don't throw out wisdom. Just because you have taken a stand on God's Word doesn't mean you shouldn't get a doctor's exam or take medicine if the Lord directs you to do it. An exam or medication won't alter your confession of faith.

It's the same way in standing on God's Word for

finances. In addition to confessing for finances – that God is going to meet all your needs – God might say, "Get up off the park bench and get a job!"

A key to patience is found in Hebrews 10:35,36:

> **Therefore do not cast away your confidence, which has great reward.**
>
> **For you have need of endurance** [*The King James Version* says, **"patience"**], **so that after you have done the will of God, you may receive the promise.**

One of the reasons you need to attend a church regularly that is preaching the uncompromised Word of God is that your faith and patience will be encouraged. Sometimes people sag in their faith and patience when they are isolated from the Body of Christ. The devil will intensify his bombardment of lies against you when you are standing alone in faith. It is also more difficult to resist the devil if the truth is not coming into your ear gate on a consistent basis.

The writer of Hebrews says:

> **And let us consider one another in order to stir up love and good works,**
>
> **Not forsaking the assembling of ourselves together, as is the manner of some, but exhorting one another, and so much the more as you see the Day approaching.**
> **Hebrews 10:24,25**

Instead of condemning one another when you see someone struggling in an area, give them a word of encouragement: "You are going to make it. Hang in there! I'm believing with you to see the full manifestation of what God has promised."

Hebrews 8:6 says, **"But now He has obtained a more excellent ministry, inasmuch as He is also Mediator of a better covenant, which was established on better promises."** Through the blood of Jesus Christ, we have a far better covenant than the first covenant God made.

The writer of Hebrews continues:

For if that first covenant had been faultless, then no place would have been sought for a second.

Because finding fault with them, He says: "Behold, the days are coming, says the Lord, when I will make a new covenant with the house of Israel and with the house of Judah –

"Not according to the covenant that I made with their fathers in the day when I took them by the hand to lead them out of the land of Egypt; because they did not continue in My covenant, and I disregarded them, says the Lord.

"For this is the covenant that I will make with the house of Israel after those days, says the Lord: I will put My laws in their mind and write them on their hearts; and I will be their God, and they shall be My people.

"None of them shall teach his neighbor, and none his brother, saying, 'Know the Lord,' for all shall know Me, from the least of them to the greatest of them.

"For I will be merciful to their unrighteousness, and

their sins and their lawless deeds I will remember no more."

Hebrews 8:7-12

When you are born again, the fulfiller of God's promises comes to live inside of you through the Person of the Holy Spirit. When you honor God's promises, you are honoring Him.

Breaking the Chains of Bondage Confession

Speak this confession aloud, believe it in your heart, and begin to act as if it is already true in your life:

It is through faith and patience that the promises of God's Word become mine. I speak in agreement with God's promises – which will never return void – rather than speaking doubt and suspicion and coming into agreement with circumstances. I'll not waver in my confession of God's promises regardless of circumstances, the opinions of others, or even of my own feelings. God's promises are mine now, and I refuse to let go of them until they manifest in my life.

Death and life are in the power of my tongue. I choose to speak life because I will partake of the fruit of my own words. I am a party to the new covenant, based upon better promises, because of Jesus' death, burial, and resurrection.

(See Hebrews 6:12, 8:6; 10:23; Isaiah 55:11; Proverbs 18:21.)

Chapter Review

As you review the teaching in this chapter, please fill in the blanks of the statements/questions below:

1. Through _____ and _____ I inherit the promises of God's Word (Hebrews 6:12).

2. Check the following items that oppose faith and the integrity of God's Word:

   ___   Doubt
   ___   Fear
   ___   Suspicion
   ___   Negative words
   ___   Positive words
   ___   Traditions of men
   ___   Feelings
   ___   Imaginations

3. The spirit of faith is to _____ and _____ the promises of God's Word (2 Corinthians 4:13).

4. My faith is growing by _____

   _____

   _____

   _____

   _____

9

KNOWING WHO YOU ARE IN CHRIST

Do you not know that the unrighteous will not inherit the kingdom of God?

1 Corinthians 6:9

There is a great deception in the world right now that says people who do evil are not going to be judged, nor is there a hell or a lake of fire. Paul said, **"The unrighteous will *not* inherit the kingdom of God. Do not be deceived..."** (v. 9).

Paul goes on and lists some of the bondages that will keep people out of heaven:

Neither fornicators, nor idolaters, nor adulterers, nor homosexuals, nor sodomites,

Nor thieves, nor covetous, nor drunkards, nor revilers, nor extortioners will inherit the kingdom of God.

And such were some of you. But you were washed, but you were sanctified, but you were justified in the name of the Lord Jesus and by the Spirit of our God.

1 Corinthians 6:9-11

Just because someone does something wrong doesn't mean they'll miss heaven. If they repent and receive the cleansing of Jesus' blood, they will make heaven.

All things are lawful for me, but all things are not helpful. All things are lawful for me, but I will not be brought under the power of any.

Verse 12

The Amplified Version of verse 12 says:

Everything is permissible (allowable and lawful) for me; but not all things are helpful (good for me to do, expedient and profitable when considered with other things). Everything is lawful for me, but I will not become the slave of anything or be brought under its power.

The whole point Paul is making is that we belong to God and to Him alone we owe our allegiance.

Some people have asked, "What's wrong with smoking cigarettes?" Smoking won't cause you to go to hell, but it will make you smell like you've been there! The bottom line for Paul was, "If Jesus is Lord, why should I let anything of this earth rule my life above Him? Jesus is Lord of every area of my life."

Foods for the stomach and the stomach for foods, but God will destroy both it and them. Now the body is not for sexual immorality but for the Lord, and the Lord for the body.

And God both raised up the Lord and will also raise us up by His power.

Do you not know that your bodies are members of Christ? Shall I then take the members of Christ and make them members of a harlot? Certainly not!

Or do you not know that he who is joined to a harlot is one body with her? For "the two," He says, "shall become one flesh."

But he who is joined to the Lord is one spirit with Him.

Flee sexual immorality. Every sin that a man does is outside the body, but he who commits sexual immorality sins against his own body.

Or do you not know that your body is the temple of the Holy Spirit who is in you, whom you have from God, and you are not your own?

For you were bought at a price; therefore glorify God in your body and in your spirit, which are God's.

Verses 13-20

When someone buys something, they own it and they have the right to dictate the policy of how it is to be used. A person in a hotel room does not have the right to remodel or refurnish it. We're not renting our body. God owns it, and He has allowed us to live in it. It is His — lock, stock, and barrel. When you understand that, then you will see why He has the right to dictate all the policy concerning your life.

When you understand that sin will keep you out of heaven, it makes the reality of getting free from every bondage even more important.

Until you realize that the bondages of sin are a violation of God's laws and you see them as God sees them, you will never deal with them appropriately.

Here are two outstanding testimonies of men who were delivered from bondage.

Jerry Henderson

"For nine years I lived in darkness, blindness, and bondage. I was what people call 'bad seed' or the 'bad apple' of the bunch. Parents didn't want their kids to hang around me.

"I started using drugs at the age of nine to try to drown out all the anger, depression, and frustration I had experienced in growing up. Not only did I smoke marijuana on a daily basis at nine years of age, but I started dealing drugs in the schools. I got expelled from school every year from sixth grade to tenth grade, and I flunked tenth grade three times with straight F's, no D's.

"By the time I was fourteen, I was a regular user of PCP, LSD, and alcohol. I'd wake up at 4:00 in the afternoon and start partying from 10:00 at night until the next morning. Then I'd sleep, wake up, and repeat the same cycle again.

"By the time I was seventeen, I was a cocaine addict. I tried to stuff drugs and alcohol into my body to cover up all the pain that was on the inside of me. Everybody thought I was Joe Cool, the average guy, but they never saw me at night. I would lie on my bed and cry out to God, even as an unbeliever, asking God to make me happy.

"At seventeen I was also sleeping on the streets after I was kicked out of my home. Later, I was kicked out of my grandma's house. You know you are bad when you get kicked out of Grandma's house!

"I broke my fist five times smashing it through windows and into brick walls, because I was so frustrated with life.

"Before I turned eighteen, I was saved at a Baptist crusade and that day many of the bondages that had me bound fell off. I then had the privilege to attend Victory Christian School where I graduated on the honor roll and was senior chaplain.

"I still had a lot of anger on the inside of me and I didn't know how to deal with it, but God worked in me until I realized it was the unforgiveness I held towards my father that held me in bondage. I love my father now. He is a wonderful man. When I made the decision to forgive my father, the anger was released.

"People look at me now and say, 'There is no way you did those things.' They are right! My old nature did. I am now a new creation in Christ Jesus!"

Wayne Smith

"Worry and fear consumed me to the point that it was affecting my wife and children. Though I didn't realize it, fear and worry had me so bound up that I wasn't even hearing from God. I was struggling in my business, which started affecting my health. I knew what was causing it, but I didn't know how to deal with it.

"In a Wednesday night church service, the Lord spoke to me, 'Wayne, give it all to Me.' I didn't understand what

He wanted, so I prayed. I said, 'Lord, You've got to show me.'

"God opened me up and started showing me things. I said, 'Lord, cleanse me. I want to do what You want.' I had a fear of man. You can't believe how much I feared man. Proverbs 29:25 says, **'The fear of man brings a snare....'** I was bound up with the constant thought, 'What will people think?'

"Thank God for Christian doctors. My doctor said, 'Wayne, worry is a sin.' It was the first time I heard this in my spirit rather than in my head. I've always heard, 'God has not given us a spirit of fear.' In fact, I had quoted that scripture at least 589 times, but I still had a spirit of fear.

"I asked God, 'Why?' He said, 'Because you haven't given it all to Me.' He said, 'Put your all on the altar. Give it to Me, and you will see Me move.' I did and He did! The biggest thing that stopped me from going to the altar for prayer was the fear of what the guys in the men's groups I teach would think.

"The three things that keep us away from God are the lust of the flesh, the lust of the eyes, and the pride of life. The pride of life was eating on me.

"Thank God for His faithfulness. He set me free from worry and fear when I responded to an altar call."

Free Indeed!

If the Son makes you free, you shall be free indeed.

John 8:36

Jesus Christ came to break sin's bondage off of our lives. That means sin no longer has dominion over us. You can willfully surrender to it, but legally Jesus has broken sin's power to rule over you. Freedom is available to all who will make Jesus Christ Lord of their lives.

The writer of Hebrews says that through Jesus' death, burial, and resurrection, He destroyed the devil's power over death and released those who through fear of death were all their lifetime subject to bondage (Hebrews 2:14,15).

First John 4:4 says, **"You are of God, little children, and have overcome them, because He who is in you is greater than he who is in the world."**

Bondages have no authority over our lives because Jesus whipped the devil, took his authority from him, and gave us the victory. It is up to you and me to appropriate this victory by *believing* and *speaking* God's Word and acknowledging the Word as our standard for all of life.

I received a letter from a prisoner who is in for life at the State Penitentiary in McAlester, Oklahoma. I want to share part of this man's letter with you to illustrate the depth of God's love that wants you to be free.

"A couple of weeks ago I was lying in my bed listening to the TV. (My TV doesn't get a full picture, only half.)"

This prisoner heard one of our one-minute TV spots. At the end of the TV spot, I give a phone number where people can call for prayer and an invitation to attend

Victory's services in the Mabee Center at Oral Roberts University.

"I can't call because I'm in prison, and I didn't hear any address given, so I listened for over a week before I finally heard it again.

"I am forty-one years old and am doing life in prison for robbery and shooting with intent. I've been in for sixteen years now. For the past four years I've been on a maximum security unit. We're allowed one hour outside a day, but I haven't been outside in the yard for over three years. You see, I just gave up and didn't care if tomorrow ever came. In fact, I hoped it wouldn't. I was continually thinking about suicide and finally this past Christmas I decided to end it all. But before I did anything, I asked God to forgive me for what I was about to do, because I didn't want the last thing I did in my life to be a sin.

"I was raised in a Baptist church as a child. I've always believed there was a God. After I said my prayer, I laid down for a couple of hours and during that time I thought I would try to make it a couple more weeks and hope that things would get better. I kept telling myself there was nothing that would make living in here any better. I don't have any family or friends on the outside, so I have no one to talk to about my feelings.

"The two weeks I had given myself were up, and then I heard your commercial. It struck something in me because you sounded sincere, like you really cared and you were talking to me.

"What I would like to know is if you or anyone from your church would like to write me and tell me more about Jesus. I could also use a friend and a good influence in my life.

"I don't want to be a bad person anymore. I remember that Jesus forgave a thief on the cross, so maybe He did forgive me last month. If He was the reason I decided to wait a couple of weeks, then I hope you are the answer I am waiting on. Please let me hear back from you or someone there."

(This prisoner has since been born again and filled with the Holy Spirit. Because of his hunger for the Word, he is being transformed into the image of Jesus Christ.)

We don't condone crime of any kind, but Jesus did forgive a thief on the cross and set him free. If you are bound and you want to be free, Jesus will set you free, too.

When I visited this man in prison after he was saved, I asked him, "What has changed in your life?" He replied, "I don't hate anymore."

Then I asked, "What is the worst thing about being in prison?" He thought for a long time and then responded, "Nothing bothers me now."

This man had a genuine born-again experience. He may be in prison, but he's now a free man. Some folks are in the free world but are still in prison. You can be free indeed by believing the truth of Jesus Christ.

Breaking the Chains of Bondage Confession

Speak this confession aloud, believe it in your heart, and begin to act as if it is already true in your life:

I have been washed, sanctified, and justified by the blood of Jesus, the name of Jesus, the Word of God, and the Spirit of God.

Jesus is Lord of every area of my life. Therefore, the works of the flesh have no place in me. Jesus broke sin's power to rule over me. Greater is He Who is in me than he who is in the world.

(See 1 Corinthians 6:11; John 8:36; 1 John 4:4.)

Chapter Review

As you review the teaching in this chapter, please fill in the blanks of the statements/questions below:

1. List the ten bondages given in First Corinthians 6:9,10 that will keep a person out of heaven:

   a. _____

   b. _____

   c. _____

   d. _____

   e. _____

   f. _____

   g. _____

   h. _____

   i. _____

   j. _____

2. You owe your allegiance to the one you have allowed to rule your life. Is Jesus your boss, or is the devil your boss? _____

3. Your body is the temple of the _____ _____ (1 Corinthians 6:19).

10

PRESSING TOWARD THE PRIZE OF THE UPWARD CALL

Not that I have already attained, or am already perfected; but I press on, that I may lay hold of that for which Christ Jesus has also laid hold of me.

Brethren, I do not count myself to have apprehended; but one thing I do, forgetting those things which are behind and reaching forward to those things which are ahead,

I press toward the goal for the prize of the upward call of God in Christ Jesus.

Philippians 3:12-14

To press toward the prize of the upward call of God in Christ Jesus, you must be free of bondages and weights.

To be bound with bondages and weights is comparable to Lazarus in his graveclothes. When Jesus called, **"Lazarus, come forth!"** (John 11:43), Lazarus came up out of the grave, but he was **"bound hand and foot with graveclothes..."** (v. 44). Jesus had a word for him, and it's also a word for you and me: **"Loose him, and let him go"** (v. 44).

Some people who have been born again are still wrapped in graveclothes – bondages from their old life still have them bound. They need to be loosed and set free. Other people have gone back to bondages from which they were delivered. The good news is, *in Jesus Christ you can be free!*

A bondage tries to exalt itself to the position of lord over your life in place of Jesus Christ, to the point it will try to dictate your thoughts, actions, and attitudes instead of Jesus dictating them. You only need one Lord and His name is Jesus. He is worthy to be Lord of all, for He is the One Who paid the complete price for your freedom.

Romans, chapter 6, deals with deliverance from the bondage of sin. Sin is the transgression of God's law and missing the mark God has set for you. It is being alienated and separated from God. It is disobedience and rebellion. That's what came into Lucifer when he was the archangel of God and led the rebellion in heaven. One-third of the angels followed him when he decided to exalt himself above God (Ezekiel 28:12-19; Isaiah 14:9-17).

Adam and Eve transgressed against God when they yielded to the devil's temptations in the garden. Because of rebellion, they lost their authority, their relationship, and their righteousness and were driven from the presence of God. As a result of their sin, the entire human race was alienated from God.

Jesus paid for our restoration back to the Father. When we receive Him as Savior and Lord, we receive the restoration He purchased for us.

Romans 6:1,2 says:

> **What shall we say then? Shall we continue in sin that grace may abound?**
>
> **Certainly not! How shall we who died to sin live any longer in it?**

Paul was asking, "Shall we continue in sin so there will be more grace and mercy?" That seems like a ridiculous question, but apparently there were people in Rome at that time who had a warped attitude.

When we accept Jesus Christ as Lord and Savior, we are alive to God and dead to sin. How much power does sin have over a dead person? If a body is dead, sin can't make it do anything. Paul was saying, "As far as that old body of sin that ruled in your life, it is now dead. Therefore, sin has no authority over you. You are like a dead person concerning sin."

Then Paul goes on to explain his position:

> **Or do you not know that as many of us as were baptized into Christ Jesus were baptized into His death?**
>
> **Therefore we were buried with Him through baptism into death, that just as Christ was raised from the dead by the glory of the Father, even so we also should walk in newness of life.**
>
> **Verses 3,4**

Paul gives two pictures to identify our freedom:

a. The picture of Jesus' death, burial, and resurrection, and

b. The picture of our baptism in water.

When Jesus Christ was raised from the dead, He had all authority in heaven and earth (Matthew 28:18). He snapped the chains of sin, seized the devil's authority, and walked out of the grave absolute Victor as a man, as God's Son. When Jesus was resurrected, He walked in total new life.

Your baptism in water after you are born again is symbolic of Jesus' death, burial, and resurrection. You are raised up to total new life. Your acceptance of Jesus' death to sin is your death to sin.

The whole process of salvation is by identification with what Jesus did. You can't die to sin by yourself, you can't raise yourself, and you can't conquer Satan by yourself. Jesus did all of this for you and me.

In water baptism, we are declaring, "Because of what Jesus did, I am now dead to sin." This was a reality in the early Church. In some of the earliest records of water baptism in the Russian church, they would wear an old robe over a brand new one. When they were baptized in water, they would remove the old robe and let it wash down the river. When you identify with Christ in water baptism, your old life is washed away. It is dead and gone.

Paul doesn't stop there. He says, **"For if we have been united together in the likeness of His death, certainly we also shall be in the likeness of His resurrection"** (Romans 6:5).

We do not leave people under water when we baptize them to make sure they are dead to sin! As they come up out of the water, they identify with Jesus' resurrection. They arise from the grave of the old life as new creations in Christ, leaving the old life behind.

It's not enough just to go through the ritual of water baptism. It is the faith and commitment that are in your heart that count, because water itself can't save you. Christ's blood saves us. Christ's blood was shed for the whole world, but only those who put faith in it will inherit the blessings of God.

> **Knowing this, that our old man was crucified with Him, that the body of sin might be done away with, that we should no longer be slaves of sin.**
>
> **Romans 6:6**

This is very similar to Second Corinthians 5:17 where Paul says, **"Therefore, if anyone is in Christ, he is a new creation; old things have passed away; behold, all things have become new."**

When you were born again, you didn't get a new brain! If you couldn't work math real good before you were saved, you probably couldn't work it any better afterwards. You didn't get a new face-lift, but maybe the corners of your mouth were lifted upward! You may look younger, because you are happier and more joyful, but you still have the same facial features. Then what was it that passed away? It was the body of sin and Satan's rulership over your old nature.

81

You may be questioning, "How is it then that a person can still sin?" You have a *choice,* just like the angels of God. In conspiracy with Lucifer, one-third of them rebelled against the Father, were kicked out of heaven and destined for the lake of fire, all because of a choice they made. Thank God we have redemption from sin in Jesus!

Paul said, **"But I discipline my body and bring it into subjection, lest, when I have preached to others, I myself should become disqualified"** (1 Corinthians 9:27). He was saying, "I keep my body under control. I don't let it do what it wants to do, but I tell it what it is going to do. My body is in subjection to my spirit. I rule it with my spirit."

When Adam was first created, his spirit was the dominant force of his life. His mind and body were under the control of his spirit. His spirit was so powerful that Adam had the supernatural ability to name all the animals. His body was created to live forever. He was alive with the life of God, and he walked in complete health.

Satan pulled at the intellect of Adam and Eve. He appealed to their physical senses. Their bodies and minds rose up and took dominion over their spirits. Man then became ruled by his mind and his body.

After I was born again, as a college student I didn't have anyone to explain it to me, but it became very clear that secular education was totally concerned about the mind, a little bit about the body, but completely neglected the spirit. There were no classes on how to love with the love of God or on the fruit of the Spirit. The most important things in life were ignored, while the mind was exalted in being taught how to make money.

When I first heard about Oral Roberts University, I heard the phrase, "spirit, mind, and body," and the concept of training the whole person. If you educate a person's mind and train their body, you've missed the main part of the person – the spirit man. Don't fool yourself that people are getting an education if their spirit is not being trained. They are getting some head knowledge and their bodies may be getting in shape, but they are not being educated in the way God planned. He wants our spirit to be fed, built up, strong, and full of the life of God.

When you are born again, Jesus Christ gives you the ability to put your body and mind where they belong and that is under the control of the Holy Spirit, Who dominates the human spirit. The mind is not changed at the new birth. It must be renewed with the Word of God.

> **I beseech you therefore, brethren, by the mercies of God, that you present your bodies a living sacrifice, holy, acceptable to God, which is your reasonable service.**
>
> **And do not be conformed to this world, but be transformed by the renewing of your mind, that you may prove what is that good and acceptable and perfect will of God.**
>
> **Romans 12:1,2**

Renewing of the mind comes through hearing the Word, reading the Bible, prayer, communion with God, and worship and praise. All of these things reveal God's thoughts, His ways, and His nature.

Once your spirit is reborn and your mind is renewed, you have to make a decision, "I am presenting my body to God, and it will be holy and acceptable unto Him." Only *you* can present your body to God and make the decision to renew your mind.

Some people who have been born again have never renewed their minds. They still have stinking thinking! Other people have renewed their mind with the Word, but their flesh still wants to hang on to some things of their old nature. There is a point where you surrender everything to God, making Jesus Lord of every area of your life.

The good news Paul is sharing is that what Christ did at Calvary is enough so you can live free from the power of sin.

For he who has died has been freed from sin.

Now if we died with Christ, we believe that we shall also live with Him,

Knowing that Christ, having been raised from the dead, dies no more. Death no longer has dominion over Him.

For the death that He died, He died to sin once for all; but the life that He lives, He lives to God.

Romans 6:7-10

Jesus came to the earth as a human being and showed

us how to live in victory. He lived in total submission to the Father.

> **Likewise you also, *reckon* [consider] yourselves to be dead indeed to sin, but alive to God in Christ Jesus our Lord.**
>
> **Romans 6:11**

Why do certain people not get free of the bondages in their lives? Some people have embraced bondages, declaring that they are dysfunctional, co-dependent, dependent upon drugs and alcohol, or they are into some form of immorality. Many times they blame it on their parents, their heritage, their environment, or the atmosphere in which they were raised.

Some people declare that they have a poverty attitude or an angry spirit. As long as you declare that you have a certain bondage, it will remain *yours*. Begin to declare, "Alcohol has no more control over me. Fear, torment, oppression, lust, envy, jealousy, and anger are dead to me." These things are part of your old, dead nature. They were put to death at the cross and put away by Jesus' death, burial, and resurrection. You identified with Him in your baptism.

Joel 3:10 says, **"Let the weak say, 'I am strong.'"** Psalm 107:2 says, **"Let the redeemed of the Lord say so, whom He has redeemed from the hand of the enemy."** Start declaring, "I am a brand new person." Some people have said, "Depression was on my grandmother, it was on my mama, and it's on me, too." As long as you are reinforcing your claim on any area of bondage, it will remain *yours* by your own confession. Proverbs 6:2 puts it this way: **"You are snared by the words of your mouth; you are taken by the words of your mouth."**

You are not reckoning yourself dead to sin if you are constantly affirming the works of the devil. While some people say, "The devil is after me," my Bible says goodness and mercy are after me! Sure, the devil comes about as a roaring lion and throws some fiery darts, but as you resist him, he will flee in terror from you. The shield of faith will stop his fiery darts.

Begin to declare, "I am free in Jesus. I am redeemed from the curse." If you have a smoking habit and you have been saying that you just can't quit, start declaring, "Cigarettes and nicotine have no authority over me." While your hand may try to sneak a pack, you can say, "No way. In the name of Jesus, I am dead to cigarettes." *Quit acknowledging that the works of the flesh have authority over you.*

If you sin, acknowledge it before God and repent of it, but don't go around saying, "The devil made me do it." Instead, you can say, "The Lord rules in my life."

> **Therefore do not let sin reign in your mortal body, that you should obey it in its lusts.**
>
> **And do not present your members as instruments of unrighteousness to sin, but present yourselves to God as being alive from the dead, and your members as instruments of righteousness to God.**

For sin shall not have dominion over you, for you are not under law but under grace.

Romans 6:12-14

Don't yield any part of your body to sin. That old mouth that used to curse can now be used to praise God. Hands that used to hit can now reach out with love and healing to others. Feet that used to run to evil can now run with the vision of God. Ears that used to listen to junk and a mind that fed on corrupt thoughts can now feed on the Word of God and the praises of the Lord.

Begin to declare, "Sin has no dominion over me. Jesus is my Lord. I renounce the devil, and I repent of every unclean thing. No work of the enemy has any rule over my life, because Jesus destroyed the power of sin and He lives in me. No bondage can rule my life, because the light of the gospel has filled my heart, giving me knowledge of God. I overcome the enemy by the blood of the Lamb and the word of my testimony. My testimony is that I am redeemed and I am blessed. Jesus is my Lord and Savior. The peace of God rules in my heart. I am free indeed."

Breaking the Chains of Bondage Confession

Speak this confession aloud, believe it in your heart, and begin to act as if it is already true in your life:

I am forgetting those things which are behind, and I am reaching forward to the things which are ahead. I am

87

pressing toward the goal for the prize of the upward call of God in Christ Jesus.

I leave the graveclothes of bondages and weights behind, and now I am clothed in God's righteousness, grace, and mercy because of Jesus' death, burial, and resurrection.

I have been redeemed from the hand of the enemy, and I am a new creation in Christ Jesus.

(See Philippians 3:13,14; Psalm 107:2; and 2 Corinthians 5:17).

Chapter Review

As you review the teaching in this chapter, please fill in the blanks of the statements/questions below:

1. I let go of the past and press forward to the things ahead that God has destined for me by _____

   _____

   _____

   _____

   _____

2. I am like a dead person concerning sin and bondage because _____

   _____

   _____

   _____

   _____

3. To me, salvation by identification with Jesus Christ means _____

   _____

   _____

   _____

   _____

4. The mind is not changed at the new birth. It must be
    renewed by _____

    _____

    _____

    _____

    _____

11

WEAPONS FOR OVERCOMING STRONGHOLDS OF BONDAGE

Through Jesus Christ, we have been given the weapons to overcome any area of bondage.

Some people have become so accustomed to chains and bondages that the thought of being free frightens them. This is true of people who have been imprisoned for many years. The key to hope and liberation is found in the Word of God.

Second Corinthians 10:3-5 says:

> **For though we walk in the flesh, we do not war according to the flesh.**
>
> **For the weapons of our warfare are not carnal but mighty in God for pulling down strongholds,**
>
> **Casting down arguments** [*The King James Version* says "imaginations"] **and every high thing that exalts itself against the knowledge of God, bringing every thought into captivity to the obedience of Christ.**

A *stronghold* is another word for "bondage," and it comes when a person yields to temptation or to an influence of the enemy, until it becomes a habit or an established pattern.

Many people who are in bondage to a chemical substance, such as alcohol or drugs, have an imagination in their mind that says, "Oh, well, it's not too bad. I can quit any time I want."

Strongholds in people's minds cause them to rationalize their habits and addictions. Paul was saying, "These imaginations or reasonings are exalting themselves above the truth of God."

When we are born again, we are to be holy and free. An imagination or a stronghold of reasoning, however, can exalt itself to a lordship position and deceive people into believing that it is okay.

Paul says we are to bring every thought into captivity to the obedience of Christ. We are to capture our thoughts and attitudes and bring them under the control and lordship of Jesus Christ.

The bottom line of whether you are in bondage or not will be revealed when you ask:

- Is it being directed by the Lord Jesus Christ?
- Is it coming from the Word of God and the Spirit of God?
- Is it coming from natural things and/or other people?

Some people are in bondage to a controlling spirit of another person. They can't move, think, or act without talking to this person and asking their direction. In this case, someone has stepped into the place of Jesus Christ. Some people can't be peaceful without popping a few pills, in which case the pills take a lordship position over Jesus Christ.

Other people are in bondage to immoral and unclean relationships, which have stepped in to take the place of their love for the Lord and a genuine love for other people.

Second Corinthians 10:6 says, **"And being ready to punish all disobedience when your obedience is fulfilled."** This means when you begin to walk in a way of freedom and there is a temptation to go another direction, you are instant to bring that thought, activity, or imagination back into control.

When you are set free, God wants you to remain free, with the ability to say "no" to those things that would lead you back into bondage.

Today is the day to make a decision, "I am going to take the weapons God has given me and pull down every stronghold the devil is trying to create as a bondage in my life. I will not walk in bondage again."

Let's look briefly at three weapons of warfare that can be used in pulling down the strongholds of bondage in your life: the blood of Jesus, the Word of God, and the name of Jesus. The power of each of these weapons is released through prayer, the confession of faith, and praise.

The Blood of Jesus

It was the blood of Jesus that redeemed us out of Satan's

authority and brought us out of the kingdom of darkness into the Kingdom of light.

Ephesians 1:7 says, **"In Him** [Jesus Christ] **we have redemption through His blood, the forgiveness of sins, according to the riches of His grace."**

First Peter 1:18,19 says:

> **Knowing that you were not redeemed with corruptible things, like silver or gold, from your aimless conduct received by tradition from your fathers,**
>
> **But with the precious blood of Christ, as of a lamb without blemish and without spot.**

To be *redeemed* means to be brought out of slavery. We were brought out of slavery, not by silver and gold, but by the precious blood of Jesus Christ. We were brought out of darkness into the Kingdom of light. As a result, we were redeemed from the curse of sin, sickness, poverty, and every type of bondage the devil would try to bring.

First John 1:7 says, **"The blood of Jesus Christ His Son cleanses us from all sin."** To *cleanse* means we are being washed and renewed continuously. We have all sinned and fallen short of the glory of God (Romans 3:23). First John 1:8 says, **"If we say that we have no sin, we deceive ourselves, and the truth is not in us."** Every person who has ever lived, except for Jesus, has sinned.

Sin brings guilt and condemnation. Out of that comes oppression, torment, and heaviness. The biggest bondage in anyone's life is sin and the consequences of it.

Jesus Christ paid the price in full for our sin with His shed blood. God accepted the sacrifice of Jesus' blood. He declared Jesus to be the King of the universe. He also declared us to be righteous when we put our trust in the work of Jesus' shed blood at Calvary.

First John 1:9 says, **"If we confess our sins, He is faithful and just to forgive us our sins and to cleanse us from all unrighteousness."** If you are going to be set free from the devil's bondages, then you must be willing to confess your sin. According to this verse, two things happen when you confess your sin:

- Jesus will forgive you, and

- He will cleanse you of all unrighteousness.

For the blood of Jesus to be effective as a weapon of warfare, your primary attitude must be a *spirit of repentance.* You apply the power of the blood, not through arrogance and pride, but through repentance, which is a deep, heartfelt sorrow for sin that causes you to turn away from it.

The book of Revelation speaks of a space of time for repentance. When repentance doesn't take place in that time frame, it's over. We have space to repent right now in this life. When we go out of this life, the time frame to repent is over. The point is, *do not play with repentance.* Don't take it lightly.

Some people are tormented because they think they have committed the unpardonable sin, yet they continue to come to the church for help. To ask for help is evidence that you haven't committed the unpardonable sin. God will forgive you.

Several years ago I was involved with an interview of a former witch on the Richard Roberts TV Program. When this woman functioned in the role of a witch before she was born again, she said the thing she feared the most was when people talked about the blood of Jesus. She said it actually paralyzed her satanic powers. Revelation 12:11 says, **"And they overcame him** [the devil] **by the blood of the Lamb and by the word of their testimony...."** There is power in Jesus' shed blood!

This is the day to declare your freedom by the blood of Jesus Christ: "By the blood of Jesus Christ, I am free from the dominion of darkness. Bondages have no more right to rule my life."

The term, *pleading the blood,* had to do with a lawyer presenting the facts of a case. When we say we are pleading the blood, we are saying that we are redeemed and completely free by Jesus' blood from all satanic influence.

The Word of God

The primary attitude you must have to use the sword of the Word effectively is *the fear of the Lord.* This means to have a reverential, holy fear of God that will cause you to turn from everything unlike Him. Proverbs 8:13 says, **"The fear of the Lord is to hate evil...."** Proverbs 16:6 says, **"By the fear of the Lord one departs from evil."**

Jesus gave us an example in Matthew 4:1-11 of using the weapon of the Word against the devil.

After forty days and nights of fasting, Jesus was tempted by the devil. Verse 3 of Matthew, chapter 4, calls Satan **"the tempter."** He tempts you to go away from God, like he did with Adam and Eve. He tempts you to disobey so he can gain dominion and authority over your life. How are you going to battle his temptations that try to bring you into bondage? Jesus resisted the tempter with, **"It is written,"** and then quoted a specific scripture that fit the situation. This is our example for overcoming the devil and his works.

When Satan commanded Jesus to turn the stones to bread to satisfy His hunger, Jesus resisted him with, **"It is written, 'Man shall not live by bread alone, but by every word that proceeds from the mouth of God'"** (v. 4).

When Satan tempted Jesus to throw Himself down off the pinnacle of the temple, Jesus again resisted him with the Word, **"It is written again, 'You shall not tempt the Lord your God'"** (v. 7).

When Satan tempted Jesus with all the kingdoms of the world he would give Him if Jesus would bow down and worship him, Jesus responded with the Word: **"Away with you, Satan! For it is written, 'You shall worship the Lord your God, and Him only you shall serve'"** (v. 10).

97

Among the weapons of warfare that Paul mentioned in Ephesians, chapter 6, is **"the sword of the Spirit, which is the word of God"** (v. 17). The weapons of our warfare aren't tanks and bombs, airplanes and machine guns. They aren't carnal, human weapons. They are the mighty weapons of God, which include the sword of the Word, the blood of Jesus, and the name of Jesus.

If you are bound with a habit or with negative thoughts, you can be free. Some people have said that they are born to be homosexuals. That's not what the Word of God says. When you accept Jesus Christ as your Lord and Savior, you have a new bloodline!

Begin to declare, "It is written, I am a new creation. It is written, I have a new Father. It is written, I have a new bloodline through Jesus Christ. Old things have passed away, and all things have become new. It is written, I have the mind of Christ. It is written, I have the spirit of power, love, and a sound mind. It is written, I bring every thought into captivity to the obedience of Jesus Christ. I think on things that are true, honest, just, pure, lovely, and of good report."

You can pray the Word, confess the Word, and praise God with the Word. An example of praising God with the Word is, "Father, I thank You that Your Son Jesus Christ redeemed us from the curse of the law. Thank You, Father, that You have lifted me up and set my feet upon the Rock, Jesus Christ."

If you are weighed down with depression or heaviness,

begin to praise God with the Word. "Lord, I thank You that You have given me the oil of joy for the spirit of mourning. You have given me the garment of praise for the spirit of heaviness." As you resist the devil with the Word, he will flee from you.

It's up to each individual to crucify or mortify his flesh. Tell it "no" and then take the sword of the Word and say, "In Jesus' name, this thing has no rule over my life. It is written, whom the Son sets free is free indeed." Confess the Word that is applicable to the particular area of bondage and give no place to the devil.

Many people pamper their flesh instead of crucifying it. When you put the flesh down, then the life of Christ will rise up inside of you. You cannot be ruled by two masters. You have to put one down and let the other be Lord of all. It's time to confess, "Jesus, You are Lord of every area of my life."

The Name of Jesus

The primary attitude you must have to use the name of Jesus effectively as a weapon of warfare is *humility*.

In Acts, chapter 19, when the seven sons of Sceva tried to use the name of Jesus to cast an evil spirit out of a man, the evil spirit answered, **"Jesus I know, and Paul I know; but who are you?"** (v. 15). Then the evil spirit **"...leaped on them, overpowered them, and prevailed against them..."** (v. 16).

The devil didn't leave at the command of the seven sons of Sceva because they were not humbly submitted to God Almighty. They weren't in relationship with God. If you are not humbly submitted to the Lord and in relationship with Him, you can speak the name of Jesus but the devil won't move.

Jesus gave us an example of humility in Philippians 2:5-11:

> Let this mind be in you which was also in Christ Jesus,
>
> Who, being in the form of God, did not consider it robbery to be equal with God,
>
> But made Himself of no reputation, taking the form of a bondservant, and coming in the likeness of men.
>
> And being found in appearance as a man, He *humbled Himself* and became obedient to the point of death, even the death of the cross.
>
> Therefore God also has highly exalted Him and given Him the name which is above every name,
>
> That at the name of Jesus every knee should bow, of those in heaven, and of those on earth, and of those under the earth,
>
> And that every tongue should confess that Jesus Christ is Lord, to the glory of God the Father.

Years ago when Sharon and I were youth pastors, a seventh grade boy who was in our youth group stopped the destruction of a tornado at his home with the name of Jesus. I happened to be at St. Francis Hospital at the time of the storm. From that site you can literally see the whole panorama of the city of Tulsa. A policeman using binoculars was monitoring the storm. He pointed and said, "There it is," and it dipped right out of the clouds. I saw the tornado come down and then go right back up in the clouds.

The seventh grade boy lived where the tornado came down. He had just returned from school, so he was home alone. He opened the sliding doors of his parents' home and looked out because he could hear and feel the storm all around. He saw the tornado which was ripping up homes in his neighborhood. We had been teaching the young people about the authority in the name of Jesus.

Steve said, "Mr. Devil, you get your tornado out of here in the name of Jesus." The tornado lifted off the ground and went back up in the clouds after destroying many homes. The home of Steve's parents was untouched.

There is authority in the name of Jesus Christ of Nazareth. There is power in that name to stop the storms that are raging in your life.

When you declare the name of Jesus as you are humbly submitted to the Lord, every bondage, imagination, and stronghold must leave you. Jesus' name has been given to you with the power of attorney. If a business person goes out of the city and wants business to go on as usual, he can confer upon another person in writing the power of attorney. The person will be named and the responsibilities, duties, and privileges he is to exercise will be spelled out so business can go on as usual.

This is exactly what Jesus did before He left earth. He assigned His work to those who believe in Him (Mark 16:15-18). He gave His name to those who believe in Him to carry on the Father's business as usual.

It's time to accept your power of attorney in the name of Jesus Christ of Nazareth and declare your freedom! This is your day of liberation! And once you are free, you can set others free!

Breaking the Chains of Bondage Confession

Speak this confession aloud, believe it in your heart, and begin to act as if it is already true in your life:

By an act of my will, I cast down imaginations, arguments, and everything that exalts itself against the knowledge of God and bring them into captivity to the obedience of Christ. In other words, I capture my thoughts and attitudes and bring them under the control and lordship of Jesus Christ.

I exercise the weapons of warfare to pull down strongholds of bondage in my life:

- *The blood of Jesus.*

- *The Word of God.*

- *The name of Jesus.*

Jesus' blood has set me free from Satan's authority and it cleanses me from all sin. Speaking God's Word with accuracy keeps me free of bondage and helps me to mature in Christ. Using the name of Jesus gives me power of attorney to declare my freedom over the devil and to keep him under my feet!

(See 2 Corinthians 10:5; Ephesians 1:7; 1 Peter 1:18,19; 1 John 1:7.)

Chapter Review

As you review the teaching in this chapter, please fill in the blanks of the statements/questions below:

1. I cast down imaginations, arguments, and everything that exalts itself against the knowledge of God by _____

    _____

    _____

    _____

    _____

2. I have been "redeemed" by the Lord Jesus Christ, which means _____

    _____

    _____

    _____

    _____

3. The work of Jesus' blood in my life includes _____

    _____

    _____

    _____

    _____

4. "The fear of the Lord" means _____

_____

_____

_____

_____

5. Jesus' example of overcoming the temptations of the devil in Matthew 4:1-11 is to _____

_____

_____

_____

_____

Personal Prayer of Commitment

Father, I refuse to be in bondage any longer to habits, possessions, and negative attitudes of the devil, the world, or the flesh. I now understand that it is in Your Son, Jesus Christ, where freedom is available simply by asking. I confess Jesus as my personal Lord and Savior and begin to renew my life with daily input of Your Word, prayer, praise and worship, and fellowship with other believers of like spirit.

I am ready to change bosses from Satan and the world to You, Lord Jesus. I am ready to move from the kingdom of darkness into Your Kingdom of light, life, and love. I believe You were crucified, buried, and resurrected to pay the penalty in full for my sin, sickness, poverty (spiritual and natural), and spiritual death.

I repent of every work of darkness, and I accept You now, Jesus, as my personal Lord and Savior. I accept the great exchange of Your nature for my old nature; of Your love for my hatred, bitterness, envy, and strife; of Your wisdom and ability for my natural ability; of Your prosperity in spirit, soul, and body for my poverty; of "heaven on earth" now as opposed to "hell on earth" where without You I have no authority to overcome the temptations and attacks of the devil.

Thank You, Lord Jesus, for empowering me with Your Spirit and equipping me to live an overcoming life of victory here in the earth now.

Today is the beginning of a new life of total victory for me, free of bondages, because You now live in me, Lord Jesus, in the Person of the Holy Spirit.

_____

(Signature)

_____

(Date)

ABOUT THE AUTHOR

Billy Joe Daugherty is the pastor of Victory Christian Center in Tulsa, Oklahoma. Present ministry outreaches include a daily radio and television ministry; and crusades held in other nations and cities.

Victory Christian Center, established in 1981, operates Victory Christian School, Victory Bible Institute, and the World Missions Training Center. With an international vision for reaching the world for Jesus Christ, Victory Christian Center has established churches and Bible schools in many nations.

Billy Joe has authored several books including *When Life Throws You a Curve, Led by the Spirit, This New Life, Principles of Prayer,* and most recently, *Living in God's Abundance,* that gives a new understanding that God has much more than we have ever dreamed or tapped into.

Billy Joe and his wife, Sharon, minister God's healing, saving and delivering power as a team. They have four children who work alongside them in the ministry.

To receive a book and tape catalog, please write to:

Victory Christian Center
7700 South Lewis Avenue
Tulsa, OK 74136-7700

109

Other Books by
Billy Joe Daugherty

When Life Throws You a Curve

Led by the Spirit

Faith Power

Building Stronger Marriages and Families:
Making Your House a Home

Demonstration of the Gospel

Killing the Giant of Ministry Debt

You Can Be Healed

Absolute Victory

This New Life

Living in God's Abundance

Books by Sharon Daugherty

Called By His Side

Walking in the Fruit of the Spirit

Avoiding Deception

For more information about the ministry
or to receive a product catalog, you may contact:

Victory Christian Center

7700 South Lewis Avenue

Tulsa, OK 74136

(918) 491-7700